D0700101

Monsters
and Mythical Creatures

Cyclops

Other titles in the Monsters and Mythical Creatures series include:

Aliens
Demons
Dragons
Goblins
Water Monsters
Zombies

Monsters
Mythical Creatures

Cyclops

David Robson

ReferencePoint
Press®

San Diego, CA

© 2011 ReferencePoint Press, Inc.
Printed in the United States

For more information, contact:
ReferencePoint Press, Inc.
PO Box 27779
San Diego, CA 92198
www.ReferencePointPress.com

LIBRARY OF CONGRESS CATALOGING-IN-PUBLICATION DATA

Robson, David, 1966–
  Cyclops / by David Robson.
    p. cm. — (Monsters and mythical creatures)
  Includes bibliographical references and index.
  ISBN-13: 978-1-60152-146-0 (hardback)
  ISBN-10: 1-60152-146-4 (hardback)
  1. Cyclopes (Greek mythology) I. Title.
  BL820.C83R65 2011
  398.20938'01—dc22
                                    2010027195

Contents

Introduction

Mysterious Skull

Three thousand years ago, perhaps more, a man living on the island of Crete in modern-day Greece was farming his land. He worked all day in the hot Aegean sun, tilling the rich soil and hoping that his spring planting of barley—a hearty grain—would result in a prosperous fall harvest. To guarantee success, he might have prayed to the gods his own parents had prayed to—powerful deities that he believed controlled every aspect of the nature that surrounded him.

One day while digging near his grove of olive trees, the farmer's shovel struck something hard buried in the ground. What he assumed was a gnarled tree root turned out to be something far more intriguing: a skull. The farmer carefully brushed the dirt and grime away and realized it was too large to belong to a human. But the skull's strangest feature was not its size; it was the gaping hole right above where the nose had been.

Did You Know?

The dwarf elephants that may have inspired the Cyclops legend lived on Mediterranean islands approximately 2 million years ago.

Like human beings throughout history, this Greek farmer and his neighbors sought to understand their world, and they drew conclusions based on a limited view of their surroundings. Although educated Greeks might have known the world was round, early myths suggest a flat earth with the Titan Atlas holding up the sky. In the stories, Greece sat in the middle of this worldly disk with Mount Olympus—meeting place of the gods—as its center. "The Greeks knew little of any real people except those to the east and south of their own country, or near the coast of the Mediterranean," wrote Thomas Bulfinch in his classic collection of Greek and Roman mythology. "Their imagination meantime peopled the western portion of this sea with giants, monsters, and enchantresses."[1]

Mysterious skull in hand, the farmer and his neighbors therefore envisioned a humanlike creature, perhaps 15 feet (4.6m) tall—a giant. The empty socket, they guessed, must have contained an eye. Because of this, they named the fearsome creature Cyclops. In Greek, *Kyklopas* combines the Greek words for "circle" and "hole." The myth of the Cyclops grew, and in time the tale spread to all corners of the Greek islands and beyond. Long before myths were written down, local storytellers would collect such yarns—even memorize them—and spin them for audiences throughout the region. At some point the Cyclops story was added to a growing list of myths featuring young men and women who battle serpent-haired Gorgons and cautionary tales starring misguided humans and gods who fly too close to the sun or steal fire and are brutally punished for it. Most important, mythology helped early peoples put their world in perspective and answer questions for which they had no clear explanations.

> ## Did You Know?
> Dwarf elephants were one-quarter the size of their more well-known relative, the woolly mammoth.

Today scientists know that the skull found so many years ago in Greece did not belong to a Cyclops. Instead, it belonged to a prehistoric beast known as *Deinotherium giganteum*, a distant, smaller relative of today's elephant. The empty hole that the ancient people believed to be an eye socket contained the trunk. Thomas Strasser, an archaeologist at California State University, Sacramento, says, "The idea that mythology explains the natural world is an old idea. The ancient Greeks . . . would certainly come across fossil bones like this

The towering one-eyed Cyclops rages at the provocations of its ancient human foes. In Greek mythology, the massive slow-witted monster combines the strength of 100 men and displays a brutal disregard for its human victims.

and try to explain them. With no concept of evolution, it makes sense that they would reconstruct them in their minds as giants, monsters, sphinxes, and so on."[2]

Although Greek mythology contains some of the most thrilling characters ever invented—Medusa, the Hydra, the Minotaur, the Sirens—few have haunted the dreams like the Cyclops. Combining the strength of 100 men with a brutal disregard for human suffering, the slow-witted Cyclops is known throughout the world. Cultures around the globe have their own versions of the beast, and its terrifying single eye has inspired movies, comic books, and novels.

> ## Did You Know?
>
> In 1879 paleontologist Othniel C. Marsh named his dinosaur skeleton discovery *Brontosaurus*, after Brontes, Cyclops of thunder.

Although the Cyclops is typically portrayed as a hideous, merciless beast, the earliest versions of the myth tell a different story altogether.

Chapter 1

Origins of the Cyclops

The ancient Greek ideal of beauty dictated that the way someone appeared on the outside was a direct reflection of one's personality on the inside, and vice versa. Greek sculptors chiseled and scraped for months to render physically beautiful specimens portraying the Greek gods. The males—like Zeus—were typically slender but well-muscled. The females were smooth bodied, their faces built around high cheekbones and supple skin.

By this Greek definition of beauty, the one-eyed giants known as the Cyclopes were some of the ranker, more despicable creatures in all of Greek mythology. Enormous, sweaty, and with a single eye sitting directly above his nose, the Cyclops was the epitome of ugliness through and through. He provided a contrast to the Greek ideal, with his slovenly exterior mirroring his inner repulsiveness. Typically a supporting character, the Cyclops, born from and dwelling in darkness, is a vital part of the Greek tradition.

Birth of the Cyclops

In Greek mythology Cyclopes have existed almost from the beginning of time. The Greek gods embodied the heavens and the earth, but before they did, there existed only a swirl of matter and uncertainty. According to Hesiod, an eighth-century B.C. Greek poet and economist, "Verily at the first Chaos came to be."[3] This comes from Hesiod's version of the dawn of the universe known as the *Theogony*, which in Greek means "birth of the gods." Like so many early creation myths, the Greek version begins in darkness:

In the beginning there was an empty darkness. The only thing in this void was Nyx, a bird with black wings. With the wind she laid a golden egg and for ages she sat upon this egg. Finally life began to stir in the egg and out of it rose Eros, the god of love. One half of the shell rose into the air and became the sky and the other became the Earth. Eros named the sky Uranus and the Earth he named Gaia [Gaea]. Then Eros made them fall in love.[4]

In the Greek creation myth, the love between Uranus (the sky) and Gaea (the earth) results in the birth of numerous children including three Cyclopes. The fearful god who imprisons his one-eyed offspring seems a far cry from the contented figure portrayed in this nineteenth-century painting, Uranus and the Dancing Stars.

The love between Uranus and Gaea, mother earth, produced 18 children: 12 of these were Titans; 3 were 100-armed, 50-headed giants known as Hecatonchires; and 3 were one-eyed creatures, the Cyclopes. But the partnership between earth and sky was already an unhappy one. Uranus despised the children Gaea gave birth to, particularly the Hecatonchires. Upon their birth, Uranus hid these offspring, named Cottus, Briareos, and Gyes, in a secret place on the earth. Gaea herself was enraged by Uranus's deed and encouraged her sons to rise up against their father. "My children, gotten of a sinful father," she said, "if you will obey me, we should punish the vile outrage of your father; for he first thought of doing shameful things."[5] But fearful of their father's wrath, none of them dared challenge him, not even the powerful Cyclopes, who, according to Hesiod's *Theogony*, "were like the gods, but one eye only was set in the midst of their fore-heads. And they were surnamed Cyclopes (Orb-eyed) because one orbed eye was set in their foreheads. Strength and might and craft were in their works."[6]

These three were named Brontes, meaning "thunder"; Steropes, meaning "lightning"; and Arges, meaning "shining one." Like some of their siblings, the first-generation Cyclopes towered above the other gods. They also possessed tremendous physical strength. As their names suggest, the Cyclopes were experts at harnessing the power of the heavens. Specifically, they had the ability to control thunder and lightning, and the three brothers worked together as blacksmiths to create fearsome, deadly weapons. So adept at their craft were these godlike creatures that as they matured, their father, Uranus, began to fear their power.

Thus, in an effort to contain the powerful Cyclopes and preserve his kingly status, Uranus kidnapped Brontes, Steropes, and Arges and imprisoned them in Tartarus, a hell-like pit beneath Hades, the

> ## Did You Know?
> One version of the Cyclops origin myth suggests that the Cyclops brothers were turned into mortals because they longed for the love of the sea nymphs Scibilia, Salicia, and Rivolia.

Greek underworld where beings travel after death. As described by the Greek poet Homer in his epic poem the *Iliad*, Tartarus is "as far beneath Hades as heaven is high above the earth."[7] Legend told that it would take a bronze anvil nine days to fall to earth from heaven; nine more days would be needed for the anvil to fall from earth to Tartarus. The place itself was encased in three layers of gloomy night, and the Cyclopes, mighty though they were, had little chance at escape.

That is until Cronos, the youngest and boldest Titan, came to their rescue. He freed his one-eyed brothers and enlisted them to help overthrow Uranus. Armed with a sharpened sickle made of stone by his mother, Cronos prepared to attack. As Uranus spread

Based on the ancient Greek ideal of beauty, sculptures such as this one usually depict Zeus, the king of the gods, as slender and well-muscled. The Cyclops, on the other hand, represents the height of ugliness with its slovenly exterior and repulsive characteristics.

night across the earth, Cronos ambushed him. The pitched battle ended with Cronos castrating, or cutting off the genitals of, his father. Uranus's spilled blood brought forth a whole host of creatures from the sea: the Gigantes, a tribe of 100 giants; the three Erinyes, goddesses of vengeance; and the Meliae, a sisterhood of ash-tree nymphs. Later Aphrodite, the Greek goddess of love and beauty, also rose from the blood-splashed waters.

Zeus Challenges Cronos

The battle over, Cronos now replaced his father as king of the gods. But like Uranus, Cronos was an insecure deity. He too feared the overwhelming strength of the Cyclopes and the Hecatonchires. And after a time, Brontes, Steropes, Arges, and their siblings were again relegated to Tartarus. To ensure that his brothers would not escape, Cronos posted the dragon Campe as guard. For his part, Uranus vowed revenge, and he and Gaea warned Cronos that his own children, not his brothers, would likely usurp his power. At first Cronos ignored this warning and, along with his sister Rhea, ruled the heavens and the earth. But this era, known today as the Greek Golden Age, did not last. Cronos began to fear his parents' prophecy. And as Rhea bore each of their children—Demeter, Hades, Hera, Poseidon, and Hestia—Cronos took the infants from their mother and ate them.

After a time, the grief-stricken Rhea was determined to stop her flesh-devouring husband. She and Gaea secretly made a plan, and when Zeus, the couple's sixth child, was born on the island of Crete, Rhea hid the child in a cave on Mount Ida. One night when Cronos came to Rhea, asking for the new baby so that he could consume him, the wily goddess gave the fiendish god a baby-sized rock wrapped in linens. Cronos swallowed the rock, known as the Omphalos Stone. According to one version of

Did You Know?

The first generation of Cyclopes are typically associated with metalworking, but the second generation appear to have few skills other than destruction.

Mount Etna: Forge of the Cyclopes

For centuries smoldering Mount Etna has fired the imaginations of people around the world. It frequently conjures images of the 3 original Cyclops brothers who, legend has it, forge weapons deep inside its belly. Roughly one-third the size of Mount Everest, the tallest mountain in the world, Etna's name appears to have originated from the Phoenician word *attuna*, or "furnace." Arabs refer to it as Jebel Utlamat, or Mountain of Fire. Etna's first recorded eruption occurred in 1500 B.C. An eruption in 122 B.C. caused so much destruction that Roman citizens of nearby Catania were exempted from paying taxes for 10 years. Today Etna's wide slopes are home to 25 percent of Sicily's population. The volcano-enriched soil on which Etna sits supports lush vineyards and orchards and subsequently the lives of thousands of local farmers. While the mountain continues spewing hot ash and belching molten lava, the slow-moving path of the lava makes human casualties rare. Still, the eruptions, which can last for more than 6 hours, are often accompanied by earthquakes that shake nearby villages and cause evacuations of thousands of people. The Cyclopes may slumber, but they rarely sleep.

the story, Rhea gave the baby Zeus to a goat named Amalthea. The animal, whose name means "tender goddess," raised the child as her own. Whenever the baby's father lurked, Amalthea enlisted heavily armored dancers to shout and clap to mask the infant's cries. Another version of Zeus's upbringing claims that a female spirit, or nymph, named Adamanthea hid the child by suspending him by a rope between the earth, sea, and sky. Still another tale suggests that Gaea, the child's grandmother, took care of the young god.

Battle for Supremacy

Once grown, according to one myth, Zeus poisoned his father, causing Uranus to vomit up the children and the stone he had consumed, one by one. In another version Zeus cut his father open to reveal his siblings. In Hesiod's *Theogony*, Zeus then traveled to Tartarus and released the Cyclopes, Hecatonchires, and creatures known as Gigantes.

As Zeus prepared to battle Cronos for absolute supremacy, Brontes, Steropes, and Arges labored mightily to provide Zeus with weaponry that would ensure victory. To that end, the Cyclopes created ear-shattering thunder to crack the sky and destructive, terrifying lightning to illuminate the heavens and rain down smoke and fire. According to the *Theogony*, "They remembered to be grateful to him for his kindness, and gave him thunder and the glowing thunderbolt and lightning: for before that, huge Earth had hidden these. In them he trusts and rules over mortals and immortals."[8]

For Zeus's brother Poseidon, ruler of the sea, the Cyclopes crafted a three-pointed metal pitchfork known as a trident. For Artemis, goddess of the hunt, they forged bows and arrows out of moonlight. And finally, for Hades, another of Zeus's brothers, the Cyclops siblings created the mysterious Helmet of Darkness, or Helm of Hades, from dog skin. The helmet could turn its wearer invisible. Later it was used by the Greek hero Perseus to slay Medusa, the snake-headed Gorgon.

Once all of the warriors were equipped, the war commenced. Known as the Titanomachy, it was fought in Thessaly, in what is now northern Greece. The Titans and Zeus's Olympians battled for the right to rule the heavens and the earth.

Victory and Destruction

After 10 years of pitched battle, Zeus and the Olympians claimed victory. Immediately, Zeus reordered the hierarchy of the gods and took his place at the top of Mount Olympus, along with his wife, Hera. Although they had been instrumental in helping to defeat the Titans, the Cyclops brothers were happy to serve Zeus and his fellow gods. Never central to the ongoing adventures of the Olympians, the one-eyed creatures provided aid and support as Zeus expanded his realm and his power.

Legend suggests that they worked under the command of Hephaestus, son of Zeus and Hera, for whom they toiled under Mount Etna, the largest active volcano in present-day Europe. There they worked to perfect Zeus's dazzling and destructive lightning bolts. As king of the gods, Zeus could be hotheaded, violent, and cruel. He often took what he wanted when he wanted it and demanded absolute loyalty and obedience from the other gods.

A Single-Eye Theory

Blacksmithing, the bending of metal to form tools, utensils, or weapons, was a common practice in early Greece. The Greeks relied so heavily on the craft that they even invented a blacksmith of the gods, Hephaestus. As a god himself, Hephaestus was supremely skilled at creating the fiercest weaponry, and he softened his magical metal on the fiery forge of Mount Etna, an active volcano. This reliance on and respect for blacksmithing may also have contributed to the earliest Cyclops myths. Walter Burkert, a professor emeritus at the University of Zurich in Switzerland, believes that the Cyclops concept might have developed among local blacksmiths and blacksmith groups thousands of years ago. At the time it was common practice for blacksmiths to wear a patch over one eye as protection from flying sparks as they banged away at their forges. How the blacksmith Cyclopes of Hesiod's *Theogony* became the flesh-chomping monster of the *Odyssey* remains unclear. One theory suggests that Polyphemus began literary life as a ferocious monster, but not until Homer's epic poem did he become a one-eyed Cyclops.

Greek mythology often includes tales of Zeus's feuds with fellow Olympians. One of those who raised the wrath of Zeus was his own son, Apollo.

The offspring of Zeus and the Titan goddess Leto, Apollo represented many things to the ancient Greeks. He was the god of light, the sun, truth, medicine, and the arts. It was said that each morning Apollo mounted a fiery chariot and, pulled by powerful horses, flew into the sky and brought daylight to the world. Like many of the gods, Apollo often mated with mortal women. He fathered a male child named Asclepius by Coronis, daughter of a Greek king.

Asclepius became a victim of Zeus's wrath after Apollo aroused the mighty god's anger by raising someone from the dead. Zeus had a firm rule against gods and humans meddling in matters of life and death.

As punishment for Apollo's crime, Zeus threw a Cyclops-made thunderbolt at Asclepius, mortally wounding him. When the youth died, Apollo became enraged. Although he had no power over his domineering father, the sun god struck at those who made the deadly weapon that destroyed his child. Apollo killed Brontes, Steropes, and Arges, or, in another version of the myth, killed sons of the Cyclopes whose names are unknown. Still, legend says that three one-eyed brothers still dwell in Mount Etna, which stands 10,922 feet (3,329m) high and is thought by scientists to be at least half a million years old. Locals say that whenever the volcano smolders, the Cyclopes are working at their blacksmith forges.

Second Generation of Cyclopes

After the deaths of the three original godlike Cyclopes, more of the one-eyed creatures mythically appeared. But now they were no longer defenders and weapon makers of Zeus. Instead, this second generation of Cyclopes remained earthbound on the Mediterranean island of Sicily, which ancient Greeks knew as Hypereia. There they dwelled in the deepest reaches of Mount Etna. The precise origin of this new crop of Cyclopes remains a mystery.

Some ancient writers suggest they were the children of Brontes, Steropes, and Arges; others believe that they too sprang from Uranus's blood after his battle with Cronos. One Cyclops, named Polyphemus, came about by neither means. Instead, according to Homer, a Greek poet from the eighth century B.C., Polyphemus was the child of Zeus's brother Poseidon, ruler of the sea, and a sea nymph named Thoosa.

Regardless of their beginnings, this group of giants was far less skilled and helpful. They appeared to have no ability to fashion

Paintings, sculptures, and mosaics (such as this one) often depict Poseidon, ruler of the seas, with his three-pronged trident. The Cyclopes crafted the trident after Poseidon's brother Zeus released the one-eyed giants from captivity.

19

potent weaponry or much of anything, for that matter. These Cyclopes lived in large caves and appeared primitive, almost animalistic. In fact, they dressed in the skins of cows and sheep and did not so much tend their land as eke out a meager existence by tending sheep and picking wild barley, wheat, and grapes. Homer describes them as having "no meeting place for council, no laws either . . . each a law to himself, ruling his wives and children, not a care in the world for any neighbor."[9]

New and Nasty

This new generation of Cyclopes was friend to neither gods nor men. According to some versions of the story, they rejected the gods because they believed themselves more powerful than the Olympians. They also segregated themselves from human civilization, and when they captured

people they either enslaved or ate them. Greek playwright Euripides wrote a version of one Cyclops legend. In the opening soliloquy a man named Silenus describes how, after he and his children were shipwrecked near Mount Etna, they were captured and forced into a life of slavery by the ugly, cruel beasts:

> We are herding a godless Cyclops's flocks; and so it is my children, striplings as they are, tend the young thereof on the edge of the downs; while my appointed task is to stay here and fill the troughs and sweep out the cave, or wait upon the ungodly Cyclops at his impious feasts. His orders now compel obedience; I have to scrape out his house with the rake you see, so as to receive the Cyclops, my absent master, and his sheep in clean caverns.[10]

Silenus was not the first, nor was he the last, human to be brutalized by this terrifying race of Cyclopes. With little respect for others, they kept to themselves. Legend suggests that even if they wanted to, they could not escape their island habitat. The Greek poet Homer wrote, "The Cyclops have no ships with crimson prows, no shipwrights there to build them good trim craft that could sail them out to foreign ports of call."[11]

Ancient Greek do-gooders could thank Zeus that the Cyclopes were stranded. Their heroic hands were already full with hideous creatures ranging from the huge, three-headed dog Cerberus to the nine-headed serpent known as the Hydra. Still, from time to time, ancient heroes tempted fate and ventured to the island of the Cyclops. By doing so, they risked life and limb, but in return they had a fearsome tale to tell that amazed their listeners and struck fear into the hearts of humankind.

Chapter 2

Adventures of the Cyclops

Readers of mythology looking for a heroic Cyclops whose loyalty, honor, and strength save the day are likely to be disappointed. In most adventures in which the Cyclops appears, he is portrayed as a huge and lumbering primitive, content to tend his flocks of sheep and goats. On occasion he curses the gods and chews on any humans he can wrap his beefy hands around. There is barely a hint of an intellect, and he is easily fooled. Unlike in the earliest Greek myths, the Cyclops of later centuries is a nasty fellow—greedy and hateful. Part human, part Bigfoot, he antagonizes the heroes and lovers who cross his path and promises to punish them for his ugliness and his cursed life.

Homer's Odyssey

The most famous tale in which the Cyclops appears is Homer's *Odyssey*, which tells the story of its hero, Odysseus, as he journeys home to the island of Ithaca from the Trojan War. "The usual hero adventure begins with someone from whom something has been taken," said the late mythology scholar Joseph Campbell. "This person then takes off on a series of adventures beyond the ordinary, either to recover what has been lost or to discover some life-giving elixir. It's usually a cycle, a going and a returning."[12]

Longing for his homeland after 10 years of war, Odysseus will have to struggle for 10 more years to reach its shores. The gods and monsters of ancient Greek mythology conspire against him. Meanwhile, his wife, Penelope, and son, Telemachus, are themselves threatened by dozens of men, the "suitors" who assume Odysseus is dead and want to marry his widow.

"Sing to me of the man, Muse, the man of twists and turns driven time and again off course, once he had plundered the hallowed heights of Troy."[13] Thus begins the epic poem the *Odyssey*. Once the war ends and Troy falls, Odysseus sets off with 12 ships stocked with sailors and supplies. Odysseus narrates book 9 of the poem, titled "In the One-Eyed Giant's Cave." The first stop on his odyssey, or long and eventful journey, is the Thracian town of Ismarus. There his deeds are anything but heroic; instead, he and his men pillage the hamlet, an event described by Odysseus this way:. "I sacked their city and slew the people. And from out the city we took their wives and much substance and divided them amongst us."[14] This brutal act leads Zeus to send a great storm, which tears the sails of Odysseus's ships to shreds and blows them off course. For nine days the tempest-tossed vessels are lost at sea, blown into an area of the sea unknown to Greek navigators.

On the tenth day, Odysseus and his crew set foot on land. The island, known as the land of the lotus eaters, is a deceptive place. Once the hero's men eat the leaves of the lotus plant, described by Homer as a "mellow fruit and flower,"[15] they become entranced and want to stay forever, forgetting home and family. Odysseus has to drag his weeping crew onto their ships, tie them to the hulls of their crafts, and row away.

Odysseus Meets Cyclops

By now Odysseus realizes that the journey home to Ithaca will be a difficult one, fraught with trials and tribulations to dwarf even the warfare he waged in Troy. Yet on they sail, ships pointed toward home, until they come to the land of the Cyclopes. Odysseus, being wise as well as brave, directs the ships to anchor in the harbor of an island from which the Cyclopes' island can be seen. This island is described by Odysseus as "thick with woods where wild goats breed by the hundreds . . . at the harbor head there's a spring that rushes fresh from beneath a cave and black poplars [trees] flourish round its mouth."[16]

At nightfall the men cannot see the Cyclopes' island, so black is the sky. But at dawn the crews of the 12 ships rise and explore the island. They hunt game with their bows and hunting spears, and "then all day long till the sun went down we sat and feasted well on sides of meat and rounds of heady wine," says Odysseus.[17] Satisfied and sleepy from food and drink, the crewmen glance over at the island of the Cyclopes and in the dimming light can see smoke from their fires, hear the bleating of their sheep and goats, and make out the gruff and heavy voices of the giants themselves. As he drifts off to sleep, Odysseus likely begins to wonder if he should venture to this mysterious place and confront the Cyclopes face-to-face.

After sleeping on it, the commander does just that. He speaks to all the crews of the 12 ships and tells them that he and his ship's men will sail across the channel and investigate the island of the giants. Homer's epic gives no reason for Odysseus's adventure to the strange island. His men have already filled their ships with food enough for months of travel. For ordinary men, tempting fate to venture to a dangerous place might be viewed as foolish, but Odysseus is no ordinary man. And he needs, some scholars argue, a challenge worthy of his skills. "In these stories," said Campbell, "the adventure that the hero is ready for is the one he gets. . . . Even the landscape and the conditions of the environment match his readiness."[18]

Ready or not, after rowing across the channel between the islands, Odysseus and his crew land on the shore and come upon a huge cavern rising above the waves. Nearby, flocks of sheep and goats are kept in pens, and around the cave are tall pine and oak trees. "Here was a giant's lair," says Odysseus. "A grim loner, dead set in his own lawless ways. Here was a piece of work, by god, a monster built like no mortal who ever supped on bread, no like a shaggy peak, I'd say—a man-mountain, rearing head and shoulders over the world."[19]

Did Homer Exist?

While the *Iliad* and its companion piece the *Odyssey* are two of the world's best-known stories, questions about Homer, their reputed author, have persisted for thousands of years. Herodotus, a fifth-century B.C. Greek historian, wrote that Homer—a blind man—lived 400 years before him. But some contemporaries of Herodotus believed that Homer existed during the Trojan War, at least 300 years earlier. Today scholars remain puzzled by conflicting evidence about Homer's life and work. After much study, eighteenth-century scholar F.A. Wolf concluded that Homer was illiterate and recited from memory the epic poetry for which he is known. But in the early twentieth century, scholar Edward C. Hegeler called the belief that one man wrote all of the work ascribed to Homer a "very doubtful proposition."[*]

Close analysis of the two works has convinced many that they were composed by the same man, but others are not so certain. Contemporary academic Martin West goes even further, saying that one, true Homer probably never existed in the first place. Homer, he wrote, is "not the name of a historical poet, but a fictitious or constructed name."[†] If true, how the works attributed to him came into being remains a mystery.

[*] Bertrand Russell, "The Philosophy of Logical Atomism," *Monist*, vol. 29. Chicago: Open Court, 1919, p. 220.

[†] Martin West, "The Invention of Homer," Classical Quarterly, Vol. 49. 1999, p. 364.

Odysseus orders most of his crew to stay on board the ship, but he chooses 12 of his best men to come with him and explore the Cyclops lair. With him, he takes a goatskin filled with delicious wine—a gift from one of Apollo's priests whom Odysseus had rescued. He and his men then make their way to the large cave, but they quickly discover that the master of the house is not at home. Inside they find flocks of sheep and goats, well cared for, and buckets full of milk and cheeses. The hungry sailors beg their captain to let them fill their sacks with food and be off. "But I would not give way," Odysseus says, "not till I saw him, saw what gifts he'd give."[20] Odysseus soon comes to regret his decision.

Trapped

Odysseus and his men build a fire, gorge on the cheeses they found, and wait for their host to return. As the sun begins to set, the Cyclops does return, herding his flocks and carrying large pieces of wood to stoke his fire. Gigantic, hideously ugly, and possessing enormous strength, the Cyclops terrifies the sailors. According to Campbell, a monster in myth is often a "horrendous presence or apparition that explodes all of your standards for harmony, order, and ethical conduct."[21]

After driving his male animals outside, he closes the entrance to the cave by slamming an enormous stone slab down in front of the opening. All is darkness, and Odysseus and his men are now trapped inside with the gigantic and terrifying creature. At first the Cyclops does not notice his visitors. Instead, he sets to work milking his goats and sheep, curdling the milk, and preparing the cheese. Only after lighting a fire does he spy his unwanted guests. "Strangers," he booms, "now who are you?"[22]

Odysseus and his men cower in fear, unable to speak. Finally, Odysseus tells the monster that he and his men were returning from Troy when they were blown off course. Invoking the name of Zeus, he begs the Cyclops for a warm welcome. But the Cyclops scoffs at the notion, and at Zeus himself, saying, "We Cyclops never blink at Zeus and Zeus's shield of storm and thunder."[23] The

Cyclops asks Odysseus where his ship is moored. The clever hero lies, saying his craft was destroyed. Just then the Cyclops grabs two sailors, smashes them on the ground like dolls, eats them, and washes his meal down with a long drink of milk. Odysseus and his men cry in horror; they are helpless. Fearing no mortal man, the Cyclops goes to sleep. Wracked with fear, Odysseus thinks to stab the monster in the chest. But he stops himself, knowing that he and his men can never push the heavy stone slab away from the cave opening.

In this sixteenth-century painting, Odysseus drives a spear into the enormous eye of the sleeping Cyclops known as Polyphemus. The monster, who has trapped Odysseus and his men in a cave, screeches in pain and cries out for help that never comes.

At dawn the Cyclops awakes, again builds a fire, and grabs two more men for his morning meal. When he leaves the cave for the pasture, he heaves the slab back in place, again trapping Odysseus and his crew inside. In the darkness Odysseus devises a plan. Near one of the animal pens, the Cyclops left his massive olivewood club. Odysseus hacks off a large chunk of it and orders his remaining men to shave it down and create a sharp point at one end. After they are finished, their leader buries the sharp end in the Cyclops's fire to harden it. Once

their weapon is ready, Odysseus has his men cover it with debris from the cave to hide it. By now all of them understand: They will stab the monster's eye out when he falls asleep. Odysseus asks for volunteers to help him complete the task; four hearty men—his best—agree.

One-Eye Returns

That evening, the ogre returns. As he did the night before, the Cyclops milks his flocks before grabbing two more sailors for his dinner. Disgusted but determined, Odysseus proceeds with his plan. Pouring the wine he had brought into a bowl, he offers it to the Cyclops. "Here, Cyclops," he says, "try this wine—to top off the banquet of human flesh you've bolted down."[24] Odysseus asks for the monster's pity. Barely listening, the Cyclops drinks the wine down and immediately demands more. He also asks for the wine giver's name so he can provide him a gift.

Odysseus fills the Cyclops's bowl two more times, until the giant begins slurring his speech and losing his wits. Then Odysseus speaks: "So, you ask me the name I'm known by, Cyclops? But you must give me a guest-gift as you've promised. Nobody—that's my name. Nobody—so my mother and father call me, all my friends."[25] The Cyclops makes good on his promise, telling Odysseus that as a gift, he will eat "nobody" last. By now the creature is exhausted and drunk and falls into a deep sleep.

Seeing his chance, Odysseus uncovers the wooden stake, bakes it in the fire to heat it, and prepares his men. He and his four helpers then lift the sharpened, red-hot spear and drive it into the sleeping Cyclops's colossal eye. Odysseus describes the deed: "We seized our stake with its fiery tip and bored it round and round in the giant's eye till blood came boiling up around that smoking shaft . . . its crackling roots blazed and hissed."[26] The monster awakes, screeching in pain. He yanks the stake from his eye, and blood gushes from the wound. He cries out for his neighbors to help. They call back to Polyphemus—the ogre's name—and ask him who has injured him. "*Nobody*, friends," he yells. "Nobody's killing me now by fraud and not by force."[27] The other Cyclopes, hearing that "nobody" has hurt him, ignore Polyphemus's plea and laugh at his foolishness.

Escape from the Cyclops

Odysseus's trick has worked, but he and his men remain trapped in the cave. Writhing in agony, the Cyclops draws back the slab from in front of his doorway, hoping that he might catch the men trying to slip out of the cave with one of his sheep. Ingeniously, Odysseus waits until the next morning and ties the sheep together in groups of three. He has each man cling to the middle beast's thick belly fleece, with the animals on either side shielding him. Odysseus himself clings to the belly of a large ram.

When the blinded Cyclops throws back the stone from his doorway, he carefully inspects each member of the flock, but he detects nothing. The hefty ram comes last. The Cyclops frisks the animal, wondering why it lagged behind the others. He imagines the old ram might be saddened by its master's gouged-out eye, and he curses "nobody" for his pain. Then he lets the ram—and the hidden Odysseus—into the pasture.

Never one to waste food and anticipating a long journey, Odysseus and his freed crew drive the Cyclops's flocks onto their ship.

A seventeenth-century painting depicts Polyphemus inspecting his sheep before releasing them into the pasture. The Cyclops does not realize until it is too late that Odysseus's men are about to escape by clinging to the bellies of the sheep.

The ship's crew greet them with shouts of gladness, but they soon cry for their lost comrades. Once at sea but within shouting distance, Odysseus taunts Polyphemus, calling him a beast and a cannibal. Enraged, Polyphemus tears off a massive piece of rock and heaves it at Odysseus's ship. The boulder lands near the ship, creating a tidal wave. Odysseus orders his men to row the ship faster to escape the mountain of water. Once again, the hero cannot help himself; he yells at the Cyclops. His men try to convince him to stop, but he will not yield. This time, he shouts his own name—Odysseus—to the angry monster, claiming responsibility for the deed that blinded Polyphemus.

The Cyclops stops, startled. He shouts back that a prophet once said he would be blinded by a man with that name. He invokes his father, Poseidon, master of the seas and god of earthquakes, to slow Odysseus's voyage home. Odysseus further curses Polyphemus and says that even Poseidon cannot bring back the Cyclops's lost eye. With that, Polyphemus calls out to his father, asking for deliverance: "Hear me, Poseidon. . . . If I really am your son and you claim to be my father—come, grant that Odysseus . . . never reaches home. Or if he's fated to see his people once again and reach his well-built house and his own native country, let him come home late and come a broken man and let him find a world of pain at home!"[28]

Polyphemus then tosses a larger boulder toward the ship. It lands close to the ship's stern, or back end. The resulting wave helps carry Odysseus's ship to the other vessels in his command. That night, he and his many men feast on the sheep they stole from the Cyclops. What they cannot know then is that Poseidon will answer his son's prayers. Odysseus will not see his homeland, Ithaca, for 10 more years.

Polyphemus the Poet

The Cyclops episode of Homer's *Odyssey* is surely the most dramatic one in which the one-eyed giant appears, but for other writers of antiquity, the character of Polyphemus proved too fascinating and horrible to leave alone. Greek poet Theocritus must have known

Homer's epic. Born in 310 B.C., he was likely raised on stories of Greek heroes like Achilles and Odysseus. Long before television and the Internet, wandering storytellers traveled throughout the Greek world weaving tales of epic battles and courageous men who overcame obstacles to win glory for themselves and for the gods they worshipped.

Today Theocritus is commonly known as the first pastoral poet. Taken from the Latin word *pastor*, meaning shepherd, pastorals are poems set in the countryside. They typically present an idealized image of rustic life among shepherds who spend much of their time wooing fair young maidens. Theocritus made his living writing such verse for sophisticated people of Alexandria, Egypt, who craved entertainment dealing with love and romance. His most famous surviving work is a series of poems, *Idylls*. Two of these include Polyphemus, the Cyclops made famous in the *Odyssey*. Yet the Cyclops portrayed in *Idylls* could not be more different from Homer's version.

> **Did You Know?**
> According to the Greek philosopher Plato, Cyclopes were not monsters but instead a race of uncivilized men.

While both retain the monster's most prominent feature—his single eye—the Polyphemus of Homer and the Polyphemus of Theocritus appear to have different personalities. Theocritus characterizes Polyphemus as a sweet shepherd, lovesick for an alluring sea nymph named Galatea. Softly, the sincere and gentle giant sings to his love, but it is of no use. She rejects his advances: "I've loved ye true," he tells her, "but Lord! to you my love as nothing is."[29]

Romantically, Polyphemus burns with passion for Galatea and only wishes he could join her beneath the sea:

"O me!
That I was not born with fins to be diving down to thee,
To kiss, if not thy lips, at least [thy] hand."[30]

Scholars have long wondered what accounts for this civilized, somewhat corny version of the Cyclops. Aside from the fact that Theocritus was writing a love poem rather than an adventure story, it may also be significant that the writer, like the mythical character, hailed from Sicily. The poet may have felt a kinship with the beastly Cyclops.

Virgil's Violent Wretch

Another ancient poet, Virgil, felt no such sympathy for Polyphemus. Born in 70 B.C. in Cisalpine Gaul (modern-day northern Italy), Virgil's father was a farmer, and it is likely that the young Roman boy knew Theocritus's work. He surely learned the story of Odysseus (the Romans called him Ulysses) and the Cyclops and used it in his own masterwork, the *Aeneid*.

The epic poem recounts the escape of Aeneas, a Trojan hero and the son of the goddess Aphrodite, from a fallen Troy. Aeneas journeys to Italy and along the way meets with heroic adventure. Eventually, according to the legend, he does battle with Turnus, an Italian prince, and subsequently founds the city upon which classical Rome was built.

Virgil's version of Polyphemus appears in an early episode of the *Aeneid*. In it Achaemenides, one of Ulysses' men, has been left behind in the cave after the blinding of the Cyclops. The abandoned sailor describes the monster's dreary den as "a house of gore and bloodstained feasts, dark and huge within."[31] Gone is Theocritus's sappy lover of a Cyclops; here, the violent wretch returns. Achaemenides recounts the bashing of his shipmates' "brains against the rocks and how Polyphemus devoured their limbs, all dripping with black blood-clots, and the warm joints quivered beneath his teeth."[32]

With pride he tells how Ulysses and his crew avenged their comrades' deaths by piercing the evil eye. But after the others escape, Achaemenides finds himself marooned on the island. He

---

Did You Know?

Nineteenth-century sculptor Auguste Rodin, most famous for *The Thinker*, created a series of sculptures based on Polyphemus the Cyclops.

Cyclopean Walls

Generations ago, people believed that certain structures were so humongous that the rocks used to build them could have only been put together by creatures as large and powerful as the Cyclops. Pausanias, a second-century A.D. geographer and traveler, provided an early firsthand account of ancient Greece and its many ruins, some of which, he claimed, were built by a race of Cyclopes. "Going on from here and turning to the right, you come to the ruins of Tiryns [a fortress]," he wrote. "The wall is a work of the Cyclopes made of unwrought stones, each stone being so big that a pair of mules could not move the smallest from its place to the slightest degree." Aristotle, the Greek philosopher, also believed that the boulders, some 26 feet (8m) thick, could not be the work of mortal men. Today's archaeologists use the term Cyclopean masonry to describe this ancient, rough-hewn stonework made of huge limestone boulders. Placed side by side and on top of one another, no mortar is used to hold the pieces together. Although scientists are now certain that Cyclopes had nothing to do with their construction, the exact methods the wall builders used remain a mystery.

Pausanias, *Descriptions of Ancient Greece: Books I and II.* London: William Heinemann, 1959, p. 383.

watches the Cyclops from afar as the giant leads his flocks of sheep to the seaside, using a pine tree as a walking stick and guide: "As soon as he touched the deep waves and reached the sea," says Achaemenides, "he washed therein the oozing blood from his eye's socket, gnashing his teeth and groaning, then strides through the open sea; nor has the wave yet wetted his towering sides."[33] Achaemenides is eventually found and rescued by Aeneas. Polyphemus hears Achaemenides sailing away and screams out so loudly that other Cyclopes rush to the waterside to see what the matter is. But it is too late. The Cyclopes stand helpless on the shoreline, unable to help their eyeless brother.

Beauty and the Beast

Ovid, a near contemporary of Virgil's, was Rome's most popular poet. His *Metamorphoses* contains nearly 250 myths drawn from Roman and Greek mythology. Born Publius Ovidius Naso in 43 B.C., the poet echoes Theocritus's lovelorn Cyclops but takes the story of the monster and the beautiful sea nymph further.

In Ovid's version, which takes place before the Cyclops loses his eye, he describes Ulysses as a "shrewd deceitful man."[34] He prefers to focus not on the epic hero's quest for home but on the pitiable Cyclops. In one passage Galatea speaks of her deep love for a youth named Acis and how she pursues him. She, in turn, is followed and harassed by Polyphemus, whom she despises. "I could not declare whether my hatred of him, or my love of Acis was the stronger.—They were equal," she says. "He [Polyphemus] is filled with passion for me. He burns hot for me, forgetful of his cattle and his caves."[35] In Galatea's telling, the Cyclops is so consumed with her that he combs his hair and trims his beard. In Ovid's time these preparations were commonplace for Roman suitors. Thus, the poet encourages his readers to sympathize with the desperate monster, at least temporarily.

Then one day, while Galatea and Acis sit together, she hears the Cyclops nearby playing a flute and singing to her. He pays homage to her beauty and asks her to stop running from him: "Galatea, if you knew me well you would regret your hasty flight from me . . . and strive for my affection."[36] He brags about the location of his cave and speaks of the plentiful fruits and

In the Roman poet Ovid's version of the Cyclops tale, Polyphemus is in love with the sea nymph Galatea but Galatea loves a youth named Acis. As seen in this painting from around the late 1500s, a jealous Polyphemus hurls a massive chunk of earth at Acis, who is buried beneath it forever.

game he has within his reach. As he finishes his song, the Cyclops spots the lovers and rages at them. Mount Etna shakes from the sound, and Galatea dives into the sea, leaving the helpless Acis alone with Polyphemus. Then, says Galatea, "the Cyclops rushed at him and hurled a fragment, he had torn out from the mountain, and although the extreme edge only of the rock could reach him there. It buried him entirely."[37]

Unable to control his rage, the Cyclops destroys the lovers' hopes for the future. In most ancient tales involving the Cyclops, he is set in opposition to the hero. Savage, but nearly sympathetic, he may play the part of villain, yet he nearly always retains a shred of humanity, however dark and twisted it might be.

Chapter 3

Cyclopes Around the World

While the Greeks may have invented the Cyclops, he does not belong to them alone. The one-eyed monster, the all-seeing eye, the ferocious fiend feasting on helpless humans or battling heroic he-men is known the world over. From the British Isles to eastern Europe to Asia, the Cyclops and his bloodthirsty brethren haunt folktales and fantasies, sagas and short stories. By whatever name he is called, his unlucky enemies nearly always fear for their lives.

Balor, the Irish Giant

Ancient Irish folklore chronicles the story of Balor, also known as the Baleful Eye. Born with a single eye into a race of giants known as the Fomorians, Balor spent his childhood on Tory Island near the county of Donegal coast. His father, King Buarainech, and mother, Queen Cethlenn, raised the boy in their ancient, earth-based religion.

Like most children, Balor was curious about the world around him and sometimes got into trouble. One night, as local druids, or ancient holy men, prepared a cauldron filled with magic herbs, Balor glanced into the brew. From then on his one eye began growing larger until it filled up much of his forehead. The eye attracted wide interest among the Fomorians, and by the time he reached adulthood, it took four men with large hooks to raise Balor's eyelid. Yet when they did, the magic eye had the power to destroy all enemies.

One enemy of the Fomorians was a race of beautiful people who loved music and poetry. Called the de Danann, or people of Dana, they were descended from the Celtic goddess Dana. In battle the de Danann stood no chance against Balor's evil eye, and Balor was crowned king of Ireland.

He enslaved the de Danann and heavily taxed what meager savings they had. Each year, the slaves were required to provide Balor with 1 ounce (28g) of gold and one-tenth of their wheat or cattle. As his parents did before him, Balor relied on the druids to foretell his future. One night, as he stood before their cauldron, the soothsayers told Balor that his future grandson would rise up, kill him, and take his place as king. Fearing for his life and his crown, Balor locked his beautiful daughter, Ethlinn, in a tall tower made of crystal and guarded by 12 loyal women. This way Ethlinn would never become pregnant and the prophecy could never come to pass. But Cian, a de Danann slave, loved Ethlinn, and aided by a druid named Birog, he sneaked into the tower dressed as a woman.

Nine months later, Ethlinn gave birth to triplets—three sons. Enraged, Balor tossed the infants into the ocean. Birog, watching nearby, dove into the sea and saved one of the babies, named Lug. Depending on which version of the myth is read, the other two children either drowned or magically turned into seals.

The Cyclops Is Defeated

Raised in exile, Lug returned at the age of 21 to claim his destiny from his grandfather. Now known as Lug the Long-Handed because of the length and power of his hands, the youth watched as Balor defeated the de Danann at the first Battle of Mag Tured. Thousands perished in an instant as the giant's eyelid was raised. Yet soon after, at the second Battle of Mag Tured, Lug wisely stood out of the evil eye's line of sight.

He waited all day and all night until Balor's eye grew tired and began to close. Then he made his move: Lug crept across the battlefield littered with bodies. Slowly, he approached the exhausted giant and crouched in readiness. Then, at the moment the eyelid was raised again but before light reached the magical pupil, Lug shot a stone from his slingshot into the fearsome eye. The hard rock flew straight to its target and with such a force that it knocked the eye through Balor's brain and out the back of his head. Twenty-seven Fomorian warriors standing behind their king were smashed to smithereens. Like the story of David killing Goliath in the Hebrew Bible, the youthful Lug had felled the terrifying giant.

Shades of the biblical tale in which David defeats the giant Goliath (depicted here in a sixteenth-century painting) can be seen in a tale from Irish folklore—with one twist. In that tale, the giant felled by the slingshot of the young hero Lug is a brutal king who also happens to be a Cyclops.

Cyclops and the Priests

Another ancient folktale, this one from Asia Minor in modern-day Turkey, twists Homer's version of the Cyclops tale. In it a priest traveled to the village to purchase a goat. Upon arriving, he met another priest who asked what he was doing. "I am going to get a goat,"[38] said the first priest. The two men journeyed to another village, and there they met a third priest who asked them the same kinds of questions. Eventually, with no goat in sight, the band of priests grew to seven.

Finally, along the road, the 7 priests met an old woman chopping wood. Suddenly, a Cyclops appeared and charged them. Before they could escape, the Cyclops captured them and dragged them to his house, which the story does not describe in detail. Yet once the Cyclops and the 7 priests arrived at the house, the single-eyed tormentor killed 1 of the priests, roasted him on a spit over his hot fire, and ate him. He washed down his meal with large gulps of wine. The other 6 priests looked on in horror, knowing full well that they would be next. But as the Cyclops got drunker, they devised a plan. With the Cyclops asleep, the 6 priests quietly crawled from their places, grabbed the spit, and drove it into the ogre's eye. With the Cyclops screaming in agony, the priests dashed from the house.

They made their way to the Cyclops's stable, where the giant kept 700 sheep. Ravenously hungry, the priests slaughtered six of the sheep and then disguised themselves by wearing the heads and tails of the animals. The next morning the wounded Cyclops entered the stable and drove his 700 sheep into the pastures. Before they passed through the stable doors, the blinded Cyclops felt the heads and tails of each sheep to make sure he did not allow the priests to escape. But escape they did, disguised as the bleating farm animals. Once inside the stable, the Cyclops stumbled across the carcasses of the sheep the priests had slaughtered.

The priests, meanwhile, led the 694 remaining sheep home to their villages. When they arrived at the home of the priest who had been murdered by the Cyclops, they gave the holy man's wife a share

Japan's Hitotsume-kozo

Folklore and superstition often coexist. In Japan superstitious people will place a bamboo basket upside down on a pole outside their houses to repel a creature known as the Hitotsume-kozo, which translates as "one-eyed rascal." Standing barely 4 feet tall and resembling nothing so much a bald-headed Buddhist monk, the Hitotsume-kozo's most recognizable feature is the large eye in the middle of its forehead. More mischievous than dangerous, the goblin has little power other than its ability to scare people. Still, some Japanese believe the creature is a bad omen and brings with it disease. To some, though, it signifies good luck.

Folklorist Yanagita Kunio studied the legend across the many islands that make up the Japanese nation. He suggests that the myth of the Hitotsume-kozo may have evolved out of ancient Japan's practice of human sacrifice. Traditionally, as village elders prepared a young person to be sacrificed to their ancient gods, his or her eye would be poked out as a way of distinguishing the person from others in society. The single eye designated the person to be sacrificed as special.

of the sheep. When the woman asked where her husband was, they told her he had stayed behind to take more sheep. On returning to their own villages, each priest kept 100 head of sheep for himself. "They ate, they drank, they attained their desires,"[39] the story concludes.

Hungarian Cyclops

Another folktale in which a hero—or heroine, in this case—works to attain a desire is Hungary's "Popelusa." The Hungarian word *popel* translates as "cinder," and "Popelusa" is an eastern European Cinderella story. In it a king has three daughters. His youngest is the most beautiful. When the king's wife suddenly dies, he marries again but soon loses his kingdom. His second wife treats the former king's daughters terribly, and before long she forces her husband to send all of the young women away.

The youngest daughter tells her sisters to unwind the three balls of thread they have so that as their father leads them into the desert, they will be able to find their way home again. They do just that, and after their father abandons them, they quickly return home. This happens twice, but the third time the daughters leave ashes instead of thread along their path. While they sleep, their father once again leaves them to fend for themselves. In the morning the girls are horrified to find that the wind has strewn the ashes far and wide. The older sisters blame their misfortune on their little sister. They taunt her and call her Popelusa. Cold and frightened, the sisters struggle to survive, and one day they are captured by a one-eyed giant, who ties them up and carries them away with him.

Upon returning to his castle, the Cyclops tells his wife to cook the two older young women. But when he touches Popelusa's arm, he finds her too skinny to make a good meal. He bids his wife to fatten the third before he feasts on her. One day, as the giant dozes, the wife departs, leaving a red-hot poker to redden in the fire. After she leaves, Popelusa encourages her sisters to take a chance and try to escape. With the giant still asleep, the elder sisters grab the red-hot poker, plunge it into the giant's single eye, and kill him. When the wife returns, they kill her too and stuff the corpses into the fire. Up to this point, "Popelusa" has echoes of more well-known fairy tales such as "Hansel and Gretel" and "Jack and the Beanstalk," but the conclusion more resembles the romance of "Cinderella." In time golden keys, fancy carriages, and a lost slipper lead to the defeat of the sulky sisters and the happy

Did You Know?

The ancient Greeks typically used the nickname "Cyclops" to refer to those who had lost an eye.

pairing of Popelusa and a handsome prince. But it is the castle of the Cyclops that provides the dingy backdrop to a story of triumph and transformation.

Searbhán and the Star-Crossed Lovers

Star-crossed lovers are again mixed up with a Cyclops-like creature in the "The Pursuit of Diarmuid and Gráinne," an Irish legend dating back to at least the tenth century. The work is part of the Fenian Cycle, one of most famous collection of tales in Irish literature. Like so many such tales, this one begins with death. Fionn, an aging warrior and leader of a group known as the Fianna, is mourning the death of his wife. He is encouraged by his men to take a new wife—the captivating Gráinne, daughter of a powerful king called Cormac mac Airt. But at a feast to celebrate their imminent marriage, Gráinne has second thoughts on the impending nuptials. Her husband-to-be is older than her father, and she cannot bear the thought of wasting her youth on Fionn.

Instead, she is attracted to a young and virile warrior named Diarmuid. To escape her bleak fate, Gráinne plies the feast guests with a sleeping potion and asks Diarmuid to run away with her. The loyal warrior refuses her advances; he is a loyal soldier and cannot betray Fionn. Angrily, Gráinne threatens Diarmuid with a treacherous spell until he relents and slips out of the castle with her. At first, they hide in a dark forest, but Fionn pursues them, vowing to take Gráinne back and make her his wife. To elude capture, the lovers hide beneath Diarmuid's stepfather's cloak of invisibility.

Guarded Berries

While on the run, Gráinne becomes pregnant and, like so many expectant mothers, begins craving particular foods. What Gráinne desires most are red rowan berries, but they are heavily guarded by a one-eyed giant named Searbhán. Diarmuid travels to the foul ogre's den and finds him sleeping. Diarmuid smacks his feet to wake him up and asks for a handful of the bitter-tasting berries to take to his beloved. Searbhán stubbornly refuses the request and curses the young couple. "I swear," says the giant, "were it even that thou shouldst have no children except that birth now in her womb . . . and were I sure that she should perish in bearing that child, that she should never taste one berry of those berries."[40]

Indignant, Diarmuid tells the giant that he will do what he must to obtain the berries and will not back down. With that, Searbhán swings his mighty wooden club and smashes the surprised Diarmuid three times. Shaken but strong, Diarmuid casts his own weapons aside and wrestles away the giant's potent club: "And when the club reached Diarmuid he struck three mighty strokes upon the giant, so that he dashed his brains out through the openings of his head and of his ears, and left him dead without life."[41] Fearing that Gráinne will see the monster's corpse, Diarmuid has Searbhán buried immediately before taking the berries to her. After she eats them, the two continue their escape from Fionn.

Eventually, the old leader stops pursuing Gráinne, and the lovers find peace in the county of Sligo, at least for a time. Diarmuid is eventually gored by a wild boar during a hunt. Fionn, also present, can save Diarmuid by letting him drink from his hands, but the vengeful old man lets the water slip through his fingers, and Diarmuid dies.

Scottish Cyclops

Searbhán is only one of many Cyclopean creatures known to the people of the British Isles. A Scottish tale from the island of Islay—allegedly told by a blind fiddler—tells of a man named Conall Cra Bhuidhe. He and his son steal a horse from the king of Lochlann, and to save himself and his child from hanging, Conall regales the king with an adventure story.

In it he says that as a boy he was hunting wild game on his father's land near the seaside. While exploring the area and its rocky terrain, he saw smoke billowing from between two rocks. He slipped and fell and upon rising caught sight of a one-eyed giant tending his two dozen goats. While he stood there in amazement, the giant approached Conall, licking his lips. "It's long since my knife is rusting in my pouch," he told the boy, "waiting for thy tender

flesh."[42] Thinking quickly, Conall convinced the hungry ogre that, being so small, he would only make one meal. He suggested that he would have more value to the giant alive because he could restore sight to the dead eye. The boy told the giant to heat the water in his great cauldron over the fire. Conall gathered stalks of heather and from it fashioned a rubbery liquid. He had the giant sit in the huge cauldron, and while the giant sat quietly by, waiting for his sight to return, the lad poured the hot rubber into the monster's good eye, blinding him. "Surely," says Conall, "it was easier to spoil the one that was well than to give sight to the other."[43]

Enraged, the monster sprang from the cauldron and blocked Conall's escape. Like Odysseus, Conall hid all night inside the creature's cave and in the morning escaped by killing a large deer kept by the monster and climbing inside its hide. When the monster released his flocks into the pasture, the disguised Conall went with them. Once outside, he taunted the Cyclops, who threw Conall a ring as a reward for eluding him. But when the young boy put it on his finger, the monster's magical ring called out for its master, who ran toward the sound. When Conall tried to remove the ring, it would not budge. In desperation he drew his knife, cut off his finger, and threw the ring into the lake. The Cyclops followed the ring into the lake and drowned. Then Conall returned to the cave and helped himself to the creature's gold and silver.

When Conall's tale is finished, he looks to the king of Lochlann for a reaction. The monarch had sentenced Conall to death

In the tale of "Hansel and Gretel," depicted in this nineteenth-century lithograph, a witch fattens a captive Hansel with the intention of cooking and eating him. A similar story unfolds in a Hungarian folktale in which three sisters are captured and readied for a meal—in this case by a Cyclops

for stealing. At first, the king gives little sign of his judgment, but slowly a smile creeps across his face. It then widens into a grin, and the king raises his glass to toast the storyteller, whose life, and that of his son, is spared.

Mongolian Marauder

One other variation on Homer's Cyclops is the Mongolian monster Depé Ghoz. This story is found in the history of a Turkic people known as the Oghuz. The tale dates back to the thirteenth or fourteenth century. In the tale a shepherd fathers a child by a fairy. The boy, Depé Ghoz, looks average in all respects but for the single eye on the top of his head. His mother gives him a ring that makes him invincible, yet she does not want him and predicts that he will terrorize his people.

The prediction comes true, as Depé Ghoz first kills his milk nurse. His first taste of flesh leaves him wanting more, and before long, dozens of Oghuz are being carried off and eaten. Local leaders amass their armies against the monster, but all are devoured. With no other recourse, the leaders try to negotiate a peace with the beast. At first, Depé Ghoz demands a ration of 12 men per day to feed his hunger, but the envoys convince him that this many people would soon deplete the population. The two sides finally settle on two men and 500 sheep each day.

> **Did You Know?**
> Serbian folklore has Psoglav, a creature with a human torso, horse legs, a dog's head, and one eye. According to superstition, the monster lived in caves and ate people.

Oghuz mothers are horrified that their sons might be next on Depé Ghoz's menu. One in particular, after losing her first son to the monster, pleads with a brave and noble warrior named Bissat to help protect her second child. Bissat agrees and determines to save his people from the senseless slaughter. Armed with a quiver of arrows and a sword, he says his goodbyes and travels to meet the giant. Upon arriving, he finds Depé Ghoz sitting on a rock. He prepares an

Cyclopes in Art

Stories, poems, and plays involving the Cyclops were so common in Greece, and the one-eyed image so indelible, that ancient artisans used it on their pottery and in their paintings. The Louvre in Paris, France, houses one such piece. Dated by archaeologists to have been created between 510 and 490 B.C., it depicts Odysseus and members of his crew driving their spear into the reclining Polyphemus's eye. Another vase shows the blinded wretch examining his sheep as Odysseus and his men cling to their bellies. Some early Roman mosaics—made of bits of colored glass and stone— also depict the Cyclops. A millennium later, painter Giulio Romano imagined Polyphemus for Renaissance audiences. His colorful portrait suggests a bearded, possibly more civilized, Cyclops, his giant club resting on his knee, a panpipe sitting in the crook of his right arm. Polyphemus looks much the same in Annibale Carracci's painted fresco from 1605. Only now he appears less than amused and has ripped a hunk of rock from a nearby mountain and is ready to hurl it at the fleeing seamen. The artists who have envisioned the Cyclops have, like so many writers, guaranteed the creature a slice of immortality.

arrow, but when he fires, it only bounces against the monster's body. A second arrow does no better. "A fly has bothered me,"[44] says Depé Ghoz. After a third try, Bissat watches as the ogre approaches him, grabs his throat, and carries the intruder to his lair. He then shoves the helpless hero into his oxhide boot and tells Bissat that he will be eaten for dinner.

Refusing to surrender, Bissat cuts himself out of the boot. He asks the giant's servant how he might kill his master. The servant tells him that only Depé Ghoz's single eye can be penetrated. So, while the monster sleeps, Bissat gouges out his eye with a heated butcher's knife. As in the other stories, the hero uses the animals to escape from the creature's cave.

A Barbarous Race

A barbarous race of ancient people, the Arimaspi were also said to have one eye in the middle of their foreheads, although unlike the typical Cyclops, the eye was average in size. Early historians Herodotus and Pliny reported that this tribe lived in a Eurasian region known as Scythia.

Flesh eating and greedy, the Arimaspi, Herodotus wrote, "were continually encroaching upon their neighbors,"[45] including a group known as the Issedonians. Another Arimaspi foe was the Griffins, mythological beings that had the head and wings of an eagle attached to the body of a lion. Traditionally Griffins are associated with the guarding of valuables and divinity, and according to this legend, the earliest in which they appear, the Griffins watched over vast stores of gold.

The Arimaspi battled the Griffins near the cave of Boreas in order to steal the valuable metal, and the wars between these two ancient factions were chronicled by Greek poet Aristeas, a near contemporary of Homer, in his epic verse *Arimaspea*. Although this work is now lost, Herodotus wrote in his *Histories* of the mysterious and unknown region, where strange people and experiences could be found: "The most outlying lands, though, as they enclose and wholly surround all the rest of the world, are likely to have those things which we think the finest and the rarest."[46] Readers of his time were all too afraid that Herodotus might be right.

A Splendid Tale

It remains unclear why the folklore of so many different cultures speaks of a Cyclops figure, although most scholars believe they all spring from the Hellenistic, or classical Greek, tradition. One collection of folktales from the early twentieth century puts it this way: "It is more probable that the Cyclops Saga is made of very ancient folk-tradition, and that later versions were shaped by the splendid imaginativeness of Homer's story."[47]

Chapter 4

The Cyclops and Popular Culture

By the twentieth century the bane of sailors, the one-eyed killing colossus, had been part of the human imagination for thousands of years. Even those who never read the *Odyssey* or did not grow up reading Greek mythology knew to fear the Cyclops. But new generations of artists were determined to reassess and reinvent ancient characters for new audiences. In some of their works, the Cyclops appears to have changed little, but in most others, the primitive beast has been transformed. Whether used as a metaphor for single-mindedness and narrow thinking or as a force for good in a world full of evildoers, the Cyclops proved to be a convenient way for writers, painters, and illustrators to express their ideas.

Cyclops in Modern Literature

During the early twentieth century, visual artists, writers, and composers sought new ways to express themselves. One writer turned to classical literature for inspiration. James Joyce grew up in Dublin, Ireland, in the late 1800s. Although raised Catholic, he eventually rejected his religious upbringing but never forgot it. Through works such as *A Portrait of the Artist as a Young Man* and *Dubliners*, a collection of short stories, Joyce developed a new and ingenious voice that would change the way people viewed literature. His novel *Ulysses*, published in 1922, took Joyce seven years to complete. Using Homer's great work as inspiration, Joyce's massive fiction tells the intertwining tale of two men, Leopold Bloom and Stephen Dedalus, over the course of one day, June 16, 1904.

The novel parallels Homer's *Odyssey* and is broken into episodes rather than chapters. Bloom, an Irish Jew whose wife is cheating on him, represents the Ulysses character, while young Dedalus symbolizes Telemachus, son of the hero. For years scholars have puzzled

Taking inspiration from Homer, author James Joyce (pictured) created Ulysses, *a massive work of fiction that parallels the* Odyssey. *One episode of Joyce's novel is reminiscent of Homer's Cyclops story, though with a more contemporary flavor.*

B Movies and the Cyclops

The early history of motion pictures is crammed with schlocky, low-budget pictures containing cheesy story-lines, bad acting, and monsters galore. Known as B movies, these movies typically played as part of a Saturday afternoon double feature at local cinemas in the 1940s and 1950s. The term B movie comes from the fact that these pictures, with fewer stars and lower production values, were not the day's feature attraction. Yet early on, B-movie producers used monsters—the Thing, the Creature from the Black Lagoon, and even the Cyclops—to sell tickets and scare audiences.

Perhaps the earliest Cyclops-related movie was 1940's *Dr. Cyclops*, in which four explorers travel to Peru, discover a supply of radium, and battle a mad scientist with poor eyesight who shrinks them down to one-fifth their normal size after they threaten to stop his twisted experiments. In 1957 Allied Artists Pictures released *The Cyclops*, which hewed slightly more closely to the Cyclops legend. After a pilot goes missing in an isolated part of Mexico, a search party that includes the pilot's fiancée travels to find him. But their plane crashes in an isolated valley populated by huge lizards, giant insects, and a 25-foot-tall (7.62m) Cyclops.

over the book, which uses a variety of writing styles and structures to convey life in turn-of-the-century Dublin.

Episode 12 of *Ulysses* suggests the Cyclops episode in Homer, but Joyce gives the episode a contemporary flavor. In it an unnamed narrator meets a friend and enters a Dublin pub for a drink. There they meet a character named Alf Bergan and another referred to only as the "Citizen," a narrow-minded Dubliner. Soon after, Bloom enters the pub and the Citizen begins chastising him, putting him down because he is Jewish and because he is indifferent to Irish politics. The Citizen in Joyce's story is the Cyclops; he can only see things in a single-minded, bigoted way. Bloom's conversation with the Citizen becomes more heated and Bloom escapes, but before he does he reminds the anti-Semitic Citizen that the Irishman's savior was himself Jewish: "Your God was a jew. Christ was a jew like me."[48] With that the Citizen hurls a biscuit at Bloom, who quickly departs.

Joyce's *Ulysses* transplanted an ancient story to the modern world and proved that the Cyclops and other mythological characters did not have to be portrayed literally. Instead, he used particular qualities found in these memorable monsters and heroes and made readers see them in new and enlightening ways.

Cyclops Goes to the Movies

With the advent of motion pictures at the turn of the twentieth century, it was inevitable that the dreaded Cyclops would eventually make an appearance. The earliest known film version of Homer's story is *The Return of Ulysses*, from 1908. Three years later this was followed by *Homer's Odyssey*. The second film, especially, includes a realistic and terrifying Cyclops sequence.

More than 40 years passed before filmmakers made another attempt to commit the most infamous Cyclops story to celluloid. In 1954 Italian director Mario Camerini made *Ulisse*. Retitled *Ulysses* for English-speaking audiences, Camerini's version of the epic saga starred American movie star Kirk Douglas as the cagey title character. The special effects by Eugen Shuftan were startling for their time. Audiences shuddered as they beheld the ghastly and gargantuan Cyclops fill his belly with hapless sailors. Played by former Olympic wrestler Umberto Silvestri, he shouts,

> **Did You Know?**
>
> In the 2000 movie *O Brother, Where Art Thou?* the Cyclops appears in the form of Big Dan, a burly Bible salesman played by actor John Goodman who is blind in one eye.

"These Greeks are stringy meat."[49] In this somewhat altered version of the tale, Ulysses and his men make the wine for Polyphemus by stomping the grapes and chanting while the amused Cyclops claps in rhythm. Film historian Jon Solomon calls *Ulysses* "the finest of all film versions of the Homeric poems."[50]

The most recent retelling was a production organized by Francis Ford Coppola, renowned director of the *Godfather* trilogy, and shown on American television in 1997. The four-hour film was directed by Andrei Konchalovsky and starred Armand Assante as Odysseus.

Bringing the Cyclops to Life

In the two most recent versions of the story, makeup artists painstakingly created a versatile piece of latex called an appliance to make the Cyclops eye a cinematic reality. To make it the artists molded a plaster version of the actor's face and then added a layer of clay to the bust, pinching it and smoothing it to look like their vision of the Cyclops. On top of that was added a coat of wet plaster. Once dried, the plaster mold of the clay face was separated from the clay version, and into the mold was poured a liquid form of latex. After it hardened, it was removed, and the artists completed their work by adding hair, paint, and most importantly, a single, bulging eyeball to the appliance.

With the makeup portion of the work completed, the actor playing the Cyclops arrived on set. As in Homer's poem, the Cyclops had to tower over Odysseus and his desperate crew. One cinematic trick used for this effect was to have the actor playing the Cyclops stand in one end of the camera frame but close by, while the others cowered at a great distance from the camera. This created the illusion of size difference.

For the more recent film version of the *Odyssey*, technicians employed computer-generated imagery (CGI). Working with a technique known as chroma key color transition, commonly referred to as green screen or blue screen, the producers first filmed the Cyclops sequences. Coached to imagine tiny sailors running

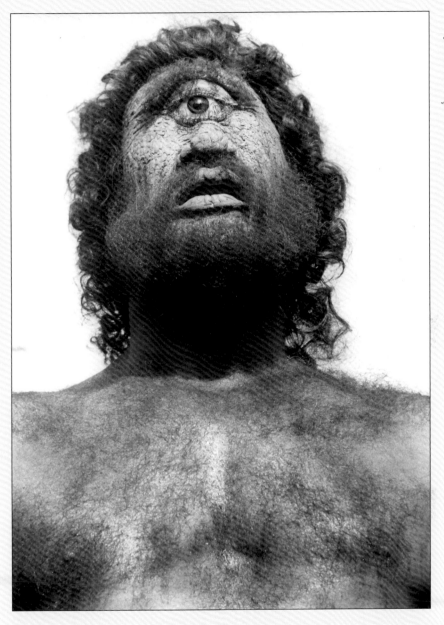

The ghastly, gargantuan Cyclops Polyphemus (pictured) was a sight to behold in the 1954 Italian film Ulisse *(retitled* Ulysses *for English-speaking audiences).* Ulysses *is the Roman name for the Greek hero Odysseus.*

in terror, the actor portraying the Cyclops cast his eye downward and spoke his lines as if he were interacting with real people. Days or weeks later, the actors playing Odysseus and his men filmed their part of the scene in front of a green screen. Behind them was nothing but a large, blank screen; they were directed to imagine a terrifying monster chasing and eating them. Once both scenes were completed, a technician fed the footage into a computer and combined them into one whole, adjusting the sizes of the actors along the way. Such work can take months of post-production to get right, but if done well, it can provide a thrilling experience for audiences.

Reinventing the Cyclops

While CGI may provide a more eye-popping Cyclops, earlier techniques such as stop-motion animation retain their charm for many contemporary movie lovers. They hearken back to a time when movies relied not on slick and showy computer-generated images but on simpler camera techniques. Stop-motion animation came into vogue in the late 1950s. During this process the animator creates the illusion of movement by adjusting a bendable model, shooting one frame of film, and then moving the model slightly more before shooting another frame. When played back at 24 frames per second—the normal speed at which a film is shot and shown—the model appears to be moving.

A pioneer of the technique is Ray Harryhausen, who got his big Hollywood break creating many of the stop-motion effects on the 1949 giant ape film called *Mighty Joe Young*. By 1958's *The Seventh Voyage of Sinbad*, Harryhausen had mastered the craft and used it to create his own unique and terrifying version of the Cyclops. In the film, Sinbad is an Arab adventurer who journeys throughout the Middle East,

> # Did You Know?
>
> The 1960s TV series *Lost in Space* included an episode in which the spaceship's crew members landed on a planet populated by a race of Cyclopes. A plastic model depicting one of the creatures holding a boulder above his head is a popular item for collectors.

Ray Harryhausen made a name for himself with his pioneering stop-motion animation techniques in the 1949 giant ape film, Mighty Joe Young. *Less than 10 years later he used the same techniques to create a unique and terrifying Cyclops in* The Seventh Voyage of Sinbad.

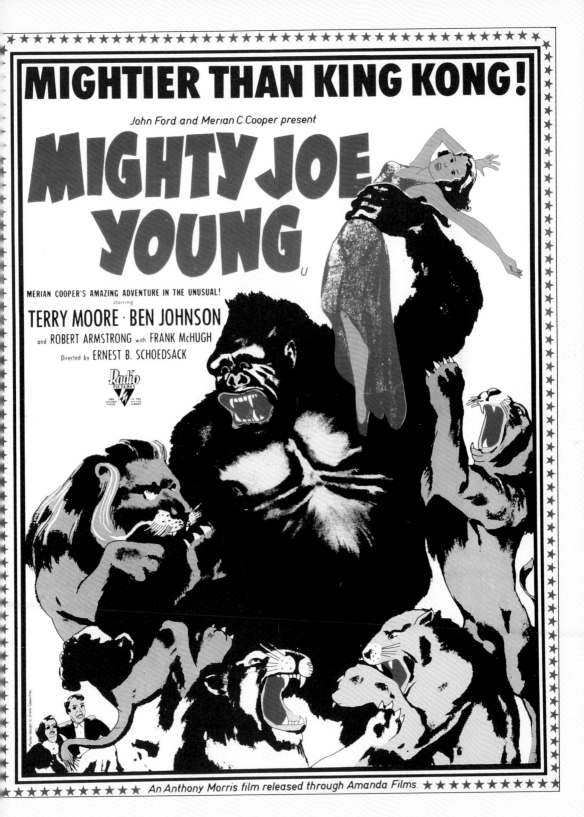

MIGHTIER THAN KING KONG!

John Ford and Merian C. Cooper present

MIGHTY JOE YOUNG

U

MERIAN COOPER'S AMAZING ADVENTURE IN THE UNUSUAL!

starring

TERRY MOORE · BEN JOHNSON

and ROBERT ARMSTRONG with FRANK McHUGH

Directed by ERNEST B. SCHOEDSACK

Radio PICTURES

Poster design © Greta Speechley

An Anthony Morris film released through Amanda Films.

East Africa, and southern Asia confronting monsters, wooing and rescuing gorgeous women, and finding riches.

Sinbad and his crew anchor near the mysterious island of Colossa. There they search for food and water and along the way come upon a giant's footprints in the sand. Curious, and less than wise, they follow the tracks to a cave whose entrance is shaped like a face. The crew's fearless leader, Sinbad, preparers to explore the cave, but before he can, a magician named Sokurah rushes out, screaming. He carries with him a magic lamp stolen from the cave's inhabitant: a Cyclops. Following him is the hideous thing itself.

Less man than beast, Harryhausen's Cyclops has hairy legs, hoofed feet, and one sharp horn on top of his head. Clearly not prone to reason or intelligible speech, the monster only growls when he attacks Sinbad and his crew. They try to repel him with spears and swords, but these are no match for the fierce creature. Later Sokurah commands the genie of the lamp to create a magical barrier between Sinbad's crew and the Cyclops. Although the crew escapes, the Cyclops throws a large boulder at them. Sinbad eventually returns to the island to do further battle with the Cyclops.

> # Did You Know?
>
> A cyclone, which uses the same word root as Cyclops, is one of the deadliest kinds of weather systems known to exist. Consisting of high intensity winds and often hundreds of miles across, the center of a cyclone is called its eye.

"The Monster to End All Monsters"

Harryhausen's favorite scene, in which the Cyclops roasts a sailor on a spit, was originally taken out of the film. "Strangely," said Harryhausen, "when the film was released in the UK [United Kingdom] the censor cut this shot because it would be too frightening for younger audiences."[51] Yet when the film was rereleased years later, the scene was restored.

To create the Cyclops, Harryhausen created three models of the monster, each a different size. In his original conception there was to

One-Eyed Monster in the Modern World

Although most people hardly notice, the Cyclops stalks the modern world, just as the Greeks believed he stalked the ancient one thousands of years ago. Today he may be harder to see and come in many forms, but he is there just the same. The Cyclops roller coaster at Mt. Olympus Theme Park in Wisconsin is made of wood and steel and begins its ride with a steep 180-degree drop. Its namesake is pictured on the side of the structure, which was built in 1995. The popular video game *Halo* includes a unit named Cyclops, and the role-playing fantasy game *Dungeons & Dragons* allows players to inhabit two types of Cyclopes. Like Ray Harryhausen's vision of the monster, these too usually have a horn jutting from their heads. Musicians have also toyed with the character. Shock rocker Marilyn Manson included a song titled "Cyclops" on his 1993 album *Portrait of an American Family*. Alternative act Terminal Power Company released a full-length album called *Cyclops* in 1995.

be a colony of Cyclopes, but time and budget concerns forced Harryhausen to scale back his plans. In his original drawing the artist envisioned a more human-looking Cyclops, but he feared that audiences would assume that men in suits were playing the Cyclops. Thus, he added the furry legs and cloven hooves, an idea he borrowed from one of his earlier creations, a creature called the Ymir, which had similar characteristics.

Because the live actors and the Cyclops were not filmed at the same time, Harryhausen employed what he called a "monster stick." The stick was roughly the size that the real creature would be, and as the actors played their parts, they could get a better sense of how tall their nemesis was supposed to be; when they looked up at him in terror it would look as if they truly had something to be frightened of.

Sam Calvin, editor of the Harryhausen-devoted fan magazine *FXRH*, believes Harryhausen's artistry remains unrivaled. "With the advent of CGI there have literally been hundreds of terrific designs in movies like *The Lord of the Rings* trilogy, the Harry Potter series, and many others. But how many of those are as memorable as the Cyclops? Harryhausen's Cyclops is the monster to end all monsters."[52]

Cyclops in the Comics

While the Cyclops may be a monster for the ages, the twentieth century saw the creature gaining a modicum of respect. In the 1930s comic books reinvented the epic hero in characters such as Batman and Superman. No doubt modeled on the Greek gods and heroes of yore, these superheroes possessed powers beyond those of mere mortals. "Comic-book heroes are the Greek gods of a modern kid's mythology," wrote *Time* magazine film critic Richard Corliss. "At once superhuman and all too human, they rise from meager surroundings to an Olympus of grandeur."[53]

Stan Lee, son of a New York City dress cutter, grew up with a love for storytelling and in time grew to love these masked and mysterious men. As a writer for Atlas Comics (later known as Marvel Comics) in the late 1950s, Lee, along with illustrator Jack Kirby, began inventing a line of now-classic characters, including Iron Man, the Fantastic Four, and Spiderman. In September 1963 Lee and Kirby developed the idea that became the X-Men. This band of mutants, led by the wheelchair-bound Professor Xavier, fight the world's evildoers. In the first X-Men comic (*X-Men* #1), Professor Xavier recruits Slim Summers (later changed to Scott Summers), a mutant able to produce a

> ## Did You Know?
>
> In the first *X-Men* movie, 6-foot-tall (1.8m) James Marsden (Cyclops) had to wear platform shoes in order to appear taller than his costar Hugh Jackman (Wolverine).

devastating and destructive "optic blast" from his eyes. When fighting crime, Summers often wears a sleek, black bodysuit and a ruby quartz visor over his eyes. The glow from the beam appears to be a single ray, and thus he is called Cyclops. Over the course of hundreds of X-Men titles, Cyclops is joined by other crime-fighting mutants, including Wolverine, Iceman, Beast, and Marvel Girl.

Cyclops Superhero

Cyclops's superhero origins were first revealed in *X-Men* #38 to #42 and later revisited in Marvel Comics' 2010 release, *X-Men Origins: Cyclops* #1. According to this contemporary comic-book mythology, Scott Summers and his younger brother, Alex, grew up in Anchorage, Alaska, the sons of U.S. Air Force major Christopher Summers.

In this scene from the 1958 film The Seventh Voyage of Sinbad, *Ray Harryhausen's Cyclops awaits his meal as an unlucky sailor roasts on a spit. When the film was released in Britain, the censor cut this scene fearing it would be too frightening for young viewers.*

One day Major Summers takes his family flying in their private plane, but soon into the flight, they come under attack by an alien spaceship. Before the plane crashes, the children's parents attach the boys to a parachute and push them from the descending aircraft. Over the course of the X-Men series, it becomes clear that Scott and Alex's parachute caught fire; during the crash landing, Scott hits his head, damaging his brain and making it nearly impossible to control his eye beams. Soon after the crash, he also develops severe headaches and takes to wearing the ruby quartz sunglasses to protect his eyes from direct sunlight. The glasses also serve to help him control the powerful rays from his eyes. After their parents' deaths, Scott and Alex become wards of the state and are separated. His inability to control his power makes Scott feel freakish, and he soon escapes the orphanage in which he lives. He wanders for a time before meeting Professor X and becoming one of the X-Men.

> ## Did You Know?
> Aside from his laserlike eye beam, the Cyclops in *X-Men* is also a black belt in judo and aikido, forms of martial arts.

Lee and Kirby, inspired by the Greek myths, transformed a hideous, one-eyed beast whose only interest was in raising sheep and eating humans into a suave and potent force for good in the world. Never before and never since has the Cyclops looked so hip. The first *X-Men* movie, released in 2000, became an enormous hit, in no small part because of actor James Marsden's vivid portrayal of Scott Summers. The Greeks made the Cyclops a legend; *X-Men* made Cyclops a do-gooder that millions of fans wanted to emulate. X-Men action figures brought the Cyclops into the homes of young children everywhere, and adults could get the Cyclops look by purchasing the dark sunglasses worn by the superhero, minus the superpower.

Standing the Test of Time

In a recent British edition of the gamer magazine *IGN*, Cyclops was chosen by the editors as the number one X-Man. The editors write:

Scott Summers has surpassed Xavier to become the greatest X-Man. A heavy burden was placed on his shoulders as a young man. He was chosen to lead a team of mutants on a crusade that would likely determine Homo Superior's [super human's] place in the world. . . . [He] defended The Dream as a knight might protect the Holy Grail. Through all of this, he's still standing.[54]

Few characters have stood the test of time like the Cyclops. First good, then bad, then supergood, his many transformations only prove the potency of the human imagination. Powerful and terrifying, the Cyclops is likely to continue exerting its hold on humans as long as there are stories to be written.

Source Notes

Introduction: Mysterious Skull

1. Thomas Bulfinch, *Bulfinch's Greek and Roman Mythology: The Age of Fable.* Mineola, NY: Dover Thrift Editions, 2000, p. 2.
2. Quoted in Hillary Mayell, "Cyclops Myth Spurred by 'One-Eyed' Fossils?" *National Geographic News*, February 3, 2003. http://news.national-geographic.com.

Chapter One: Origins of the Cyclops

3. Hesiod, *Theogony* 2.116–38. Trans. H.G. Evelyn-White. Greek Mythology. www.greekmythology.com.
4. Williams College Computer Science Department, "Greek Creation Myth," 2010. www.cs.williams.edu.
5. Hesiod, *Theogony* 2.164–66.
6. Hesiod, *Theogony* 2.139–46.
7. Homer, *The Iliad.* Trans. Samuel Butler. Radford, VA: Wilder, 2007, p. 77.
8. Hesiod, *Theogony* 2.492–506.
9. Homer, *The Odyssey.* Trans. Robert Fagles. New York: Penguin Classics, 1996, p. 215.
10. Euripides, *The Cyclops.* Trans. E.P. Coleridge. Internet Classics Archive, 1994–2009. http://classics.mit.edu.
11. Homer, *The Odyssey*, p. 215.

Chapter Two: Adventures of the Cyclops

12. Joseph Campbell with Bill Moyers, *The Power of Myth.* New York: Doubleday, 1988, p. 123.
13. Homer, *The Odyssey*, p. 77.
14. Quoted in Joseph Campbell, *Occidental Mythology: The Masks of God.* New York: Penguin, 1976, p. 164.
15. Homer, *The Odyssey*, p. 214.

16. Homer, *The Odyssey*, p. 215.

17. Homer, *The Odyssey*, p. 216.

18. Campbell with Moyers, *The Power of Myth*, p. 129.

19. Homer, *The Odyssey*, p. 217.

20. Homer, *The Odyssey*, p. 218.

21. Campbell with Moyers, *The Power of Myth*, p. 222.

22. Homer, *The Odyssey*, p. 219.

23. Homer, *The Odyssey*, p. 220.

24. Homer, *The Odyssey*, p. 222.

25. Homer, *The Odyssey*, p. 223.

26. Homer, *The Odyssey*, p. 223.

27. Homer, *The Odyssey*, p. 224.

28. Homer, *The Odyssey*, p. 228.

29. Theocritus, *Idylls 5-11*, Theoi Greek Mythology. www.theoi. com.

30. Theocritus, *Idylls 5-11*.

31. Virgil, *Aeneid 3*, Theoi Greek Mythology. www.theoi.com.

32. Virgil, *Aeneid 3*.

33. Virgil, *Aeneid 3*.

34. Ovid, *Metamorphoses*. Theoi Greek Mythology. www.theoi. com.

35. Ovid, *Metamorphoses*.

36. Ovid, *Metamorphoses*.

37. Ovid, *Metamorphoses*.

Chapter Three: Cyclopes Around the World

38. Quoted in Richard McGillivray Dawkins, *Modern Greek in Asia Minor: A Study of the Dialects of Sílli, Cappadocia and Phárasa, with Grammar, Texts, Translations and Glossary*. Ann Arbor: University of Michigan Library, 2010, p. 551.

39. Quoted in Dawkins, *Modern Greek in Asia Minor*, p. 551.

40. Celtic Literature Collective, "The Pursuit of Diarmuid and Grainne." www.maryjones.us.

41. Celtic Literature Collective, "The Pursuit of Diarmuid and Grainne."

42. Quoted in Eric Csapo, *Theories of Mythology*. Hoboken, NJ: Wiley-Blackwell, 2005, p. 58.

43. Quoted in Csapo, *Theories of Mythology*, p. 58.

44. Quoted in Csapo, *Theories of Mythology*, p. 58.

45. Herodotus, *The History of Herodotus*. Trans. George Rawlinson. London: John Murray, 1875, p. 11.

46. Herodotus, *Histories* 3.116.1, Theoi Greek Mythology. www.theoi.com.

47. Joseph Jacobs et al., *Folklore*. Vol. 19. London: Folk-Lore Society, 1908, p. 174.

Chapter Four: The Cyclops and Popular Culture

48. James Joyce, *Ulysses*. New York: Vintage, 1986, p. 280.

49. Quoted in Jon Solomon, *The Ancient World in the Cinema*. New Haven, CT: Yale University Press, 2001, p. 108.

50. Solomon, *The Ancient World in the Cinema*, p. 108.

51. Ray Harryhausen and Tony Dalton, *Ray Harryhausen: An Animated Life*. New York: Billboard, 2004, p. 116.

52. Curt Hardaway and Sam Calvin, "Is Ray Harryhausen's Cyclops the Greatest Monster in Movie History?" Monster Kid Online Magazine #7, 2008. http://gammillustrations.bizland.com.

53. Richard Corliss, "Kick-Ass: Redefining the Superhero," *Time*, April 26, 2010. www.time.com.

54. Hilary Goldstein and Richard George, "The Top 25 X-Men," *IGN*, 2010. http://uk.comics.ign.com.

For Further Exploration

Books

Megan E. Bryant, *Oh My Gods! A Look-It-Up Guide to the Gods of Mythology*. Danbury, CT: Franklin Watts, 2009.

Olivia Coolidge, *Greek Myths*. New York: Houghton Mifflin, 2008.

Euripides, *Cyclops*. New York: CreateSpace, 2009.

Ray Harryhausen, *The Art of Ray Harryhausen*. New York: Watson-Guptill, 2008.

Homer, *The Odyssey*. Trans. Robert Fagles. New York: Penguin Classics, 1999.

Sophia Kelly, *What a Beast! A Look-It-Up Guide to the Monsters and Mutants of Mythology*. Danbury, CT: Franklin Watts, 2009.

Anne Pearson, *Ancient Greece*. New York: DK Children, 2007.

Bruce Thornton, *Greek Ways: How the Greeks Created Western Civilization*. New York: Encounter, 2002.

Web Sites

Ancient Greek Mythology (www.greekmyth.org). Developed and maintained by classics professor Anthony Bulloch, this exhaustive and well-organized site is a must-see for any serious study of Greek mythology. Running the Grecian gamut from Achilles to Zeus, this site provides scholars and students alike with a host of images, analyses, and links related to their favorite ancient figures.

Greek Mythology (www.greekmythology.com). This site is devoted to providing brief but clear descriptions of the major Greek deities. It also includes quick and easy links to major Greeks texts, including the *Odyssey*, the *Iliad*, and Hesiod's *Theogony*.

Mythweb (www.mythweb.com). Geared to a younger audience, this site is useful for both students and teachers. Users can search Greek myth terms or explore heroes and gods of the ancient world by clicking on their images. Mythweb provides a friendly introduction to the subject.

Theoi Greek Mythology (www.theoi.com). This visually beautiful resource explores ancient myth through literature and art. Users can search the Greek gods' family trees or scroll through classical artistic renderings of the immortals. Check out the Greek vase painting gallery and see how the Greeks portrayed Zeus, Hera, or Artemis.

Women in Greek Myths (www.paleothea.com). Dedicated to exploring and appreciating the females of Greek myth, this site divides its subjects into goddesses, nymphs, mortals, Amazons, and monsters. Reproductions of gorgeous artwork accompany each well-written and detailed description.

Index

Note: Boldface page numbers refer to illustrations.

Picture Credits

Cover: Scala/Art Resource, NY

Bildarchiv Preussischer Kultarbesitz/Art Resource, NY: 11, 46

© Corbis/David Lees: 36

iStockphoto.com: 13, 19

© Look and Learn/The Bridgeman Art Library International: 8

National Portrait Gallery, London, UK/© DACS/The Bridgeman Art Library International: 53

Photofest: 57, 59, 63

Réunion des Musées Nationaux/Art Resource, NY: 40

Scala/Art Resource, NY: 27, 31

About the Author

David Robson's many books for young people include *Encounters with Vampires* and *The Devil.* He is also an award-winning teacher and playwright whose work for the stage has been performed across the country and abroad. Robson was introduced to Greek mythology as a boy by his grandfather and through the work of classicist Edith Hamilton. He lives in Wilmington, Delaware, with his family.